Legal Weapon

by Mark Wheeller

dbda

Legal Weapon
by Mark Wheeller

"Legal Weapon" was commissioned by:
Bedfordshire, Berkshire, Buckinghamshire, Cambridge, East Sussex, Essex, Hertfordshire, Isle of Wight, Kent, Oxfordshire, Surrey, Suffolk and West Sussex County Council Road Safety Departments.

Author's acknowledgments:
Ian Harris, Principal Road Safety Officer, Oxfordshire County Council Road Safety Group; Mandy Rigault, Senior Road Safety Officer, Oxfordshire County Council Road Safety Group; Mike Pill, Area Commander, Oxfordshire Ambulance Service, NHS Trust; Meg Davis of MBA Literary Agents; Tony Audenshaw and Matt Kane of Ape Theatre Company for their imaginative ideas to improve on my original script.

All the characters in this play are fictional although accounts of Road Traffic Accidents/ Offences are devised from those with first hand experience of Road Traffic Accidents.

Published by *dbda* in 1999
Reprinted 2002

ISBN 1 902843 01 0

BRITISH LIBRARY CATALOGUING IN PUBLICATION DATA
A catalogue record for this book is available from the British Library.

All enquiries regarding all rights associated with this pay, including performing rights, should be addressed to:
Meg Davis, MBA Literary Agents Limited, 62 Grafton Way, London W1P 5LD.
Tel: 020 7387 2076   Fax: 020 7387 2042   E-mail: meg@mbalit.co.uk

Further copies of this publication can be purchased from:
dbda, Pin Point, 1-2 Rosslyn Crescent, Harrow HA1 2SB.
Tel: 0870 333 7771   Fax: 0870 333 7772   E-mail: info@dbda.co.uk

Introduction by Mark Wheeller

If I am asked to write a Road Safety play, I always jump at the chance. There is lots of scope for dramatic moments, fast action and opportunities to utilise a variety of dramatic conventions and presentation techniques. By their very nature, they require an imaginative response to write and stage the climatic accident scenes. Beyond that there is a great sense of satisfaction and fulfilment in knowing that in addition to them being "exciting theatre" they do help to reduce accidents and save lives.

Legal Weapon arose out of a request from Mandy Rigault and Ian Harris from Oxfordshire County Council Road Safety Department to write a play about the dangers of speed. Their phone call came to me out of the blue and was the first time I'd been "commissioned" to write a play... to be performed primarily by school or Youth Theatre Groups. A number of other counties subsequently chose to become involved in the commission. I was over the moon!

The main rule I have applied to writing my Road Safety plays is that they should be good stories, and open to imaginative presentation. They should be plays that I, as a Drama teacher, would want my GCSE groups to benefit from seeing. The (crucially important) Road Safety element should add to an already interesting story and set of character relationships.

Mandy Rigault organised some interviews with people who had been convicted of serious road traffic accidents where speed was a contributory factor. The interviews were planned to happen on one day. By lunch time I was feeling a bit down... each of the three people who had come forward to talk to me stressed that their main charge had been drink/driving. The ideas were therefore covering the same ground as those explored in *Too Much Punch For Judy.* After lunch, a very confident and charming young man walked into my interview room keen to tell his story. He applied the most unexpected argument to the circumstances of his accident. Although he openly admitted he was speeding (70 miles an hour in a 40 zone), he claimed that he did not **cause** the accident which led to the death of a motorcyclist. In his view the motorcyclist was responsible for her own death because she pulled out of a junction... without looking. He was very eloquent in his justification and was able to gloss over the fact that, according to the investigation, it was unlikely that she would have been able to see him when she looked in his direction before pulling out. His speed was such that he would not have been visible over the brow of a hill. Although upset

Introduction

by the death, he was more upset about being in prison. It was the experience of prison that would stop him from ever speeding again.

This unexpected perspective provided me with the main body of the story. I sat at my word processor and invented a love triangle story (which I had never done before and wanted to try) assimilating road safety messages into that structure. I also had another objective; to create a scene which could be used by GCSE drama students to present in their final performance exam. Section 4 of the play attempts to fulfil this. The final conflict between Andy, Jazz and Matt was written with the GCSE requirements in mind: five minutes per performer, with a cast of more than two. That part of the play is 15 minutes long approximately, and has good roles for one female and two male actors.

The play was due to be premiered by a number of schools from the commissioning Counties on the same day. One of the schools (my old school St. John's, in Epping, Essex) somehow got permission to do a private performance the week before the official premiere, so that by a strange quirk of circumstances I saw that version first. I was invited to watch it in the same Drama studio as **Too Much Punch For Judy** had first been performed under my direction nearly ten years previously.

This performance was excellent. There are many bits that I had forgotten about and so, at times, I was pleasantly suprised by the script as well as the little touches that had made sections "come alive". My main reaction was: "Wow! That's a relief! It does hang together... it does work!".

The following year my own Youth Theatre membership requested to do the play. My relationship with the play became much closer during our rehearsal period and I made a number of changes.

One major challenge is staging a car accident with limited resources. I remember that I had brought eggs and melons to the rehearsal with the vague notion that battering them with a piece of metal would somehow represent the idea of metal hitting flesh. Try as we might... none of these ideas worked out! Suddenly we hit upon the idea of Andy actually beating Kelly (the motorcyclist) up... on and on... mercilessly... relentlessly... in the same way that a car will continue on its path no matter what is in its way. Andy was in control of the car, so in essence it was he who was driving this metal at Kelly. We found a way of staging the initial impact and then followed it up with a merciless slow motion one-on-one beating. The idea worked brilliantly and I can remember going home very excited about it.

4

When a week later I went to see the *Ape Theatre Company's* professional premiere, I discovered they had used a similar way of conveying the violence of the accident. How both groups came up with such a "new" idea, working in two different parts of the country... I shall never know!

Ape Theatre Company (who continue to tour **Too Much Punch For Judy** so successfully after ten years) took on the professionally touring rights to this play throughout England. Tony Audenshaw and Matt Kane, the directors of *Ape* proposed a change which I couldn't imagine working. It has since become one of my favourite aspects of the play. Their idea was to open the play with a seemingly irrelevant snippet of conversation, taken from the middle of the script. I could not see any way to make this work until I saw the *Ape* performance. The idea was excellent and I immediately adopted it and drafted it into the script.

The *Ape* production was way beyond my expectations. What I really liked about it was how much they'd added to the script without actually changing the words. This is best exemplified by their use of vocal sound effects made throughout the play to create various atmospheres and moods. There are so many other examples I could give. I was absolutely gob smacked! If you have seen their touring production you will know exactly what I mean. I consider myself to be very fortunate indeed to have had the opportunity to see my work enhanced by top professionals... and this version of the script benefits enormously from their input.

Coming back to the play three years after its conception to prepare for its publication has been a joy. Elements of the play pleasantly surprised me... and some of it even made me laugh. I've made a few more alterations for this, the published version of the play. I hope it finds its way into lots of School/College Drama departments and onto lots of school stages.

Good luck with any work you choose to do with it.

List of Characters

"A"

Andy Bowen	Male
Jazzy Maihnah	Female
Matt Irvine.	Male
Clowns or Masked Actors:	A minimum of two actors can be used in this scene. There is no prescribed maximum!
Actors portraying film:	Again any number of actors can be used in this section of the play. They would probably be the same as above... but need not be!

Car salesperson

Kelly McFarlane

Brian or Cath McFarlane   Kelly's mum or dad

Police 1 & 2

Judge

"B", "C" & "D"

Neighbours 1 & 2

Paramedics 1-3

D.I. Morris

Prisoners 1 & 2.

With doubling this play can be presented by 2 male, 2 female with parts allocated as follows:

Male 1:	A, B, C & D (when appropriate); Andy Bowen; Clowns/Masked Actor; Actor in film
Male 2:	A, B, C & D (when appropriate); Matt Irvine; Brian McFarlane; Clowns/Masked Actor; Actor in film; Police 1; Salesperson, Paramedic 1; Judge; Prisoner 1
Female 1:	A, B, C & D (when appropriate); Jazzy Maihnah; Clowns/Masked Actor; Actor in film; Neighbour 1-3; Witness; Judge; Prisoner 2
Female 2:	A, B, C & D (when appropriate); Kelly McFarlane; Clowns/Masked Actor; Actor in film; Police 2; Paramedic 2 & 3; D.I. Morris; Prosecutor; Judge; Prisoner 3 (taking some of the lines from Prisoner 1 & 2)

This play should be performed with minimum props
and maximum imagination!

The professional premier of this play was
by Epping based Ape Theatre Company
in January 1996.

The cast was as follows:

Andy: Shaun Dooley
Jazz: Julie Nicholson
Matt: Kyle Harris
Cath: Susan Mitchell

Directors:

Mat Kane & Antony Audenshaw

Section 1:   Love's Young Dream

(A slide, or a banner stands at the back of the stage. it reads:
"Human blood is heavy; the man that has shed it can not run away."
African proverb.

(This should be in view as the audience walk in to the auditorium. It can remain in view throughout the whole play but should be spot-lighted throughout the whole of Section 4 and as the audience leave.)

Kelly:	*(Wearing outdoor clothes. Preparing to go out, putting a coat and rucksack on. Calling as though upstairs where Dad/Mum is ironing.)* Dad/(Mum)!
Brian (or Cath):	*(Entering)* What?
Kelly:	Can you lend me a fiver to get some petrol for my moped ... interview at the supermarket. Remember?
Brian (or Cath):	Forgot ... sorry.
Kelly:	I'll pay you back when I get my job!
Brian (or Cath):	*(Getting the money from his/her wallet)* What happens if you don't?
Kelly:	I will. He already said he liked the look of me!
Brian (or Cath):	You watch him. *(S/He gives Kelly the money)*
Kelly:	Thanks Dad/Mum. *(Kisses him/her. Picks up (from A?) a cheap and much used motorcycle helmet.)* I'll be back as soon as I can ... just after five I guess.
Brian (or Cath):	Good luck Kelly. *(Freeze)*
A:	Kelly MacFarlane ... sixteen year old Boldly on her way where all have gone before A-knocking ... on the rat-race door.

Clowns/Masks enter and present a comedy mime scene showing the rush to get to work in the morning. (The more imaginative the mime the better!) The use of character masks could be considered.
Clowns/Masks should feel free to accompany movements with either appropriate pre-recorded or live music, vocal sound effects and/or

gobbledygook speech. Feel free to develop this opening idea. The aim is to start off with a bang! It must be lively!)

A: "A hasty man drinks his tea with a fork".
(Clowns perform an appropriate mime quickly, then look at A confused.)
Driving too fast kills around 1,000 people every year. Remember; if you drive too fast; you could be a killer ...

Car engine sounds begin - vocal or pre-recorded. Two Clowns/Masks rush across the stage and bang into each other. Both fall over. Only one gets up. The other remains on the floor.)

Disposing of someone by crashing into them is very easy, although there are other effective ways of committing murder:

(Two Clowns/Masks come forward. One has a huge inflatable club. The other is unarmed. UNARMED walks around nonchalantly. CLUBBER, tiptoeing behind him/her clubs UNARMED who falls to the ground. CLUBBER continues to club UNARMED mercilessly. Meanwhile GUNMAN - dressed in Western gear, or with appropriate music in background - creeps up behind CLUBBER. CLUBBER finishes clubbing, checks that UNARMED is dead. Puts his/her club down, brushes hands together, turns and is shot by GUNMAN with a very loud shotgun.)

This, of course, is only pretend *(The Clowns/Masks come back to life.)* In real life it is advisable not to kill people. If you do ... *(One Clown/Mask strangles another)* you can expect to be outcast by the rest of society ... *(Mime showing how - perhaps a variety of ways in which - the other clowns outcast STRANGLER)*

No, it's much more fun to *(Pre-recorded orchestral music floats in and the Clowns/Masks change their mood)* ... fall in love ... *(mime: Clowns/Masks falling in love)*

This happens to the central character in our play ...

we'll call him Andy *(Enters, as the Clowns/Masks exit.)* and the current object of his desire ... Jazz. *(Enters. Silence. Mime.)* Each time they encounter one another, their pupils dilate *(Mime)* and strange feelings pass through the whole ... yes the whole of their body. *(Mime!)*. Finally, they pluck up the courage to ask each other out. *(Simultaneously both take a breath to ask the other out.)*

Both: I ... *(They both stop. Embarrassed silence.)*

Jazz: Yeh?

Andy: I ... erm ... I don't really know why I'm here? ...

Jazz: What?

Andy: I thought you were about to ask me why I'm here!

Jazz: No.

Andy: Cos ... well you see I was just beamed up here.

Jazz: Beamed up?

Andy: Yeh. One minute I was sitting eating my lunch ... the next "Pow!" I'm here! Weird eh?

Jazz: Very weird!

Andy: Never happened before ... just "Pow!"

Jazz: "Pow?!"

Andy: "Pow!" ... Well, Actually Jazz, no!

Jazz: No?

Andy: I walked here. *(Indicating legs)* On these ... both of them ... like this. *(Demonstrates a "walk".)* I came here on purpose.

Jazz: And?

Andy: I came to ask you ... *(Clearing his throat, preparing for asking her out)* How ... *(finally chickens out)* ...

Aaaargh!

A: Trying to ask someone out is, arguably, not much more fun than being killed ... *(Another murder in the background?)*

Jazz: Do what?

A: Come on. Big deep breath and ...

Andy: Jazz please don't go. *(Suddenly becoming very melodramatic)* There's something I need to say to you.

Jazz: Are you trying to ask me out?

Andy: I've been waiting for the right moment ... and ... I think now is that moment. Jazz ... *(Suddenly double taking on Jazz's previous line)* What did you say?

Jazz: If you're trying to ask me out the answer's yes!

Andy: What, me?

Jazz: Where do you want to go?

Andy: *(Andy fumbles, stutters, stammers for a long time as though he is about to come up with all sorts of ideas, before saying quite decidedly!)* You choose.

Jazz: Clubbing?

Andy: My dancing's embarrassing, People say I look like a Telly Tubby* on acid. *(Appropriate over the top mime!)* How about Bunjee jumping?

Jazz: *(Laughing)* I can't even do long jump!

Andy: It's a laugh! I know! A meal ... oh you're not on a diet are you ... not that you need to be ... I mean ... *(Trying hard to extricate himself)* No ... let's not go out for a meal.

Or other topical cultural reference.

Section 1

A:	What are they going to do?
Andy & Jazz:	*(Very loudly)* Aaaaargh!
A:	Idea! *(Tongue in cheek)* Ping!
Andy & Jazz:	*(To each other)* How about the Cinema? "Really Scary Movie II" (?) is on! Yeh! *(Ensure title relates to the film actually seen. See section below, where Jazz and Andy are in the Cinema.)*
Andy:	I'll pick you up ...
Both:	Seven o' clock. Date! *(Jazz Exits)*
Andy:	*(Fx Atmospheric sound.)* A motorbike is a very attractive, very macho thing. Throttle up and you're away. You feel that you're on your own and nothing else in the world is relevant. The brute power all there and you're in control of it. It's the element of taming that power I like. The feeling that you're on the edge of control.
A:	The edge of control? Seven fourteen that evening ... Andy arrives with the neighbours' curtains twitching, *(Separate faces appear from different points/levels from behind curtains/screens all over the stage area)* as his monstrous machine throbs outside her home.
Jazz:	My dad'll be having a fit!
Andy:	I bet you weren't expecting a "ride" on something as big as this tonight?
Jazz:	*(Laughing.)* I've ridden bigger!
Andy:	Size isn't everything!
Jazz:	So long as it handles well.
Andy:	I can coax it in the most slippery of conditions.
Jazz:	*(Tapping watch)* Shame it couldn't get you here on time!

12

Andy:	I was actually round my Grandad's.
Jazz:	Your Grandad's?
Andy:	Nan died, about a month ago ... he needs the company.
Jazz:	That's really sweet of you.
Andy:	*(Laughing off the compliment)* He's more like a dad to me. I've helped him do up cars ever since I was a twinkle in my dad's pants! *(Passing motorbike helmet to Jazz.)* Come on ...
Jazz:	What time does the film start? Quarter to?
Andy:	Half-past.
Jazz:	*(Looking at watch in horror)* Will we make it?
Andy:	No problem!
Andy & Jazz:	Morphin time! *(They both morph into "Biker Rangers"* ... suitably over the top with appropriate musical accompaniment.)* Leathers!
Andy:	Davidson Power! *(Appropriate mime)*
Jazz:	Suzuki Power! *(Appropriate mime)*
Andy & Jazz:	Helmets on!
Andy:	Ignition *(Fx ignition)*
Andy & Jazz:	Throttle. *(Engine roars.)* Go!!! *(Possible use of pre-recorded music, as they speed off on the bike)*
Jazz:	*(Sudden transition.)* Wow! What a ride!
A:	*(As soon as A speaks the slow motion stops.)* Into the Cinema a darkened auditorium To entertain their mutual sensorium.

(A small group of actors - can include Jazz and Andy - should devise a very short scene showing a popular film genre, i.e. horror, love, murder etc.

---

*Or other topical cultural reference.

Section 1

reduced to one or two minutes, taking care not to infringe any copyright - by stealing actual film stories or for that matter trademarked names! The acting style must be lively, fast and humourous. Have fun with it!)

Both:	*(Excitement and enthusiasm)* What a film! What an evening! What a start to a beautiful relationship! *(Put on helmets. Vocal quality implies bad news to follow)* What a journey home!
Andy:	*(Looking at watch, Musing)* Ten minutes to get here. We can make it home in eight and a half!
Jazz:	What?
Andy:	Just a little game ... *(Subtle use of atmospheric fx. To be said with significance. Turning to audience. All on-stage except A are in slow motion.)* ... it adds interest to the journey.
A:	Little game?
Andy:	It's a battle ... a battle between the bike, the road and me.
A:	And other road users?
Andy:	The race instinct. It's not unusual. *(Fx off. Slow motion returns to normal speed.)*
Police 1 & 2:	Nee nah! Nee nah! Nee nah! Nee nah!
Andy:	Old Bill!
Police 1 & 2:	'Ello 'ello 'ello 'ello! What's going on here then?
Andy:	*(Taking off helmet. Jazz leaves hers on.)* Just driving home after a good evening out Officer.
Police 1 & 2:	Not been drinking I hope.
Andy:	No Officer. I don't drink and drive.
Andy & Jazz:	*(To audience)* That's dangerous!
Police 1 & 2:	You seem to be in a bit of a hurry? What sort of

speed do you think you were doing?

Andy:	Oh ... normal sort of speed for this road, Officer. Built up area. ... Thirty?
Police 1 & 2:	*(They look at one another)* Professional are you?
Andy:	What?
Police 1 & 2:	Comedian! *(They laugh together then suddenly turning on Andy and becoming very menacing)* This says you were doing 50.
Andy:	*(In a very high pitched voice)* Fifty? Me?
All:	Nicked!
Police 1 & 2:	Fixed penalty. £XX:00*. *(They exit)*
Andy:	Bastards! That's my second ... next one's an automatic ban!
Jazz:	What are you going to do?
Andy:	I'm going to have to be much more careful ...
Jazz:	Good!
Andy:	... careful not to get nicked again!
A:	Let's take a look inside Andy's mind To see if we can find some kind .... of wisdom ... *(Jazz freezes as "A" mimes opening Andy's head ... then uses him as a ventriloquists dummy) ...* Ah ha! Here we are!
(& Andy?):	"50's not fast, 50's not criminal. 50 in a 30 is pretty unexceptional. The police should prioritise use of their time. Murders, rapes, robberies ... solve "proper" crime... Take police off traffic duties they're needed elsewhere So I can drive fast without pigs in my hair!" *(Andy switches back to Andy and "A" moves away)*

*Establish what the current fixed penalty is.

Section 1

Jazz:	How are you gonna pay the fine?
Andy:	Grandad'll sort that, he did last time. He won't want it to worry my mum.
Jazz:	You're not taking it very seriously are you? Anything could have happened.
Andy:	I thought you were enjoying it!
Jazz:	*(Provocatively)* I wouldn't say it satisfied me ... entirely! *(They strike up a suitably provocative freeze)*
A:	Ten weeks on They're still going strong Summer Hols arrive and they decide to go away To stay At a Camp for a week. Andy's pretty serious and Jazz's so content That when asked to do a Bungee jump she gives her full consent!
Andy & Jazz:	Butlins! *(Perhaps some recent summer pop music can provide an atmosphere in the background for the "Butlins sequence" until "Bereavement" where it stops suddenly. Again this sequence should be as lively as possible!)* Bargain break!
A:	*(Mocking)* Bognor!
Andy & Jazz:	*(Both enjoy)* Bingo and Bowling. *(Jazz enjoys, Andy is bored by:)* Betting at the bookies.
A:	*(Takes the bear to Andy)* Bernie the Bear for ...
Andy:	*(Self adoringly)* ... best looking bloke ... *(Jazz pretends to be sick)*
Andy & Jazz:	*(Both enjoy)* Bathing on the beach! Barrels of beer and bopping to the bygone bands in the bar.

16

A:	Bereavement. *(Silence)*
Jazz:	Your Grandad's in hospital ...
A:	Some people, broke in ... and he disturbed them ...
Jazz:	It seems like he's in a bad way Andy. Sorry.
A:	Holiday curtailed they dash back home to Surrey How relevant are speed limits to someone in a hurry?

(Becomes pastiche sports commentator ... Murray Walker(?) ... with appropriate fx?) Well Good afternoon from the A24 where the bulk of this afternoon's race is to take place. I've never seen Andy Bowen look so determined. He says he's going all out to win this one - so we have, in prospect a superb sprint race! They're off!

Bowen is away first, surging ahead, ignoring the traffic lights, and, oh my goodness there's a Citroen ZX which screeches off the track allowing Bowen through completely unscathed. And again we see the dangers of such a lot of vehicles squabbling for the small amount of available road.

Over the cross roads without looking, through the chicane, and on to the motorway intersection which has claimed so many riders in practice. Bowen slows, cautious at first, and, oh my goodness! Magnificent!

Straight into the fast lane ... he must be doing well over a hundred, impressive riding on such a small bike and it has to be said a very brave ride by his pillion Jazzy Maihnah. Ignoring the clenched fists of other competitors Bowen speeds through the town centre and straight into the hospital car park. And, oh my goodness there's an ambulance right in his path, but he's up on a ramp and ... yes he's over it!!

What a barnstorming grandstand finish! Who can

	possibly fault the skill of this talented rider? He richly deserves everything that's coming to him after that ride! Now, lets go live to the hospital waiting area and try to snatch a quick word with what must be an elated Andy Bowen.
Andy:	*(To Jazz, with a very serious tone)* We didn't get here quick enough. He died about ten minutes before we got here ... heart attack.
Jazz:	Andy ...
Andy:	The doctor said his physical damage was minimal, but ... well ... he was so scared that ... he was literally scared to death. They think it was kids. *(Pause)* Jazz, if we hadn't gone away none of this would have happened.
Jazz:	It's stupid to say that.
Andy:	I'd've been there.
Jazz:	You mustn't blame yourself.
Andy:	They'd've seen my bike and they wouldn't have broken in.
A:	An affluent OAP ... obvious target, but all they managed was twenty quid and a bit of jewellery.
Andy:	He never kept money in the house. If they'd found it they'd've just left and he wouldn't have been killed ... and after Nan as well ...
Jazz:	I loved watching you two together.
Andy:	How do people who do things like that manage to live with themselves?
Jazz:	I guess they're so cold they just blank it out ...
Andy:	I didn't even get a chance to say good-bye to him.
Jazz:	You couldn't have got here any quicker..

Andy:	Yeh ... but Grandad doesn't know that ... all he knew was that I was on holiday ... I wanted him to know that ...
A:	There's no resolution to that today So we'll speed along the highway of this play, To see bad news turns to good Like it always should. *(Gives Andy the envelope)* The inheritance from your Grandad. For a young lad Such money can be dangerous.
Andy:	*(Opening the envelope and looks carefully at the enclosed cheque)* What! I don't believe it! Twenty-five thousand quid. Twenty-five grand?
A:	*(As "A" speaks, Andy accompanies the words with appropriate actions/reactions)* He splashes out on Driving Lessons, and passes the test first go; With a bucketful of dough He makes for the local Car Showroom ... .
Andy:	I want a car that's cool
Salesperson:	*(Indicating 'ideal' car)* Anyone ignoring this one, has to be a fool.
Andy:	I want a car with power, I want a car for speed.
Salesperson:	Ah! Look no further ... this is the one you need. Complete with driver's airbag and ABS brakes, Crash bars and crumple zones for your high speed mistakes.
Andy:	Nice ... but it must have tinted windows, metallic paint, five spoke alloys and a CD multiplay!
Salesperson:	You can't go wrong with this high performance, top of the range, all singing, all dancing air conditioned Cabriolet!

Good price ... you won't find any better no matter where you try
Trust me mate ... I'm a car salesman ... I never lie ... Honest!
Oh ... and how about this, a touch-tone - yours to own -
Irresistible "Can't look cool without it" Mobile Phone! I'll throw it in for "free" ...

Both: *(Shaking hands)* Deal!

Andy: Done!

Salesperson: You have been! *(Exits)*

Jazz: *(Entering)* Smart! Really cool!

Andy: Thought you'd like it. Come on ... let's go for a spin.

Jazz: Excellent!

Andy: Garage forecourt ... clock right ... left ... right ... wheelspin onto the main road ... cross-roads ... Speed limit ... 30! ... speed up to fifty ... motorway exit one mile further ... test her out ...
Speed camera sign ... *(under breath)* bollocks! ... thirty ... nice and innocent ... slip road ... motorway ... empty .. yes!!! ... accelerate ... power ... 0-100 in x seconds here we come! ... pratt in the outside lane doing eighty ... flash him ... hoot him!
Drive right up his arse and yeh ... he's got the message ... flick the V's overtake and touch on 130 miles per hour ... and pose pose pose ...
(Jazz enters)

A: They tear off through the village ... an OAP waves his stick
And a kid innocently crossing a Zebra turns a shade anaemic
Jazz you'd better hide your eyes you won't want to know
And while you're not looking ...

Andy & A:	Pump up the stereo.
Jazz:	You know what they say Andy ... blokes who drive fast are only compensating for the size of their manhood!
Andy:	What's my reason then?
A:	The motorway ... outside lane cruising at ... well I don't know what And steaming up behind them, a Sierra ... comes into eyeshot ...
Andy:	"What the hell's he up to?"
Jazz:	Who?
Andy:	There's some idiot coming up behind us doing well over a ton and he doesn't look like he's going to slow down.
Jazz:	Can't you just pull over.
Andy:	"No, I've got to get past this old biddy. Hold tight!"
A:	Foot down on the gas ... Sunday afternooner is easy to pass Slickly Andy switches to the inside lane, And takes a look in the mirror again, And horror of horrors ... what does see ...
Andy:	The self same Sierra trailing ... me.
Jazz:	What's up?
Andy:	You're not going to believe this!
Jazz:	Go on!
Andy:	I think it's an unmarked police car and he's pulling me over ...
Jazz:	What?
Andy:	I was trying to keep out of his way! I'm well and truly screwed up now.

Section 1

Jazz:	You'll be banned!
Andy:	Cheers for the helpful reminder Jazz!
Police 1 & 2:	'Ello 'ello 'ello 'ello! What's going on here then?
Andy:	I was actually trying to get out of your way Officer.
Police 1 & 2:	Professional are you?
Andy:	No Officer ... I'm not a professional comedian ... nor do I have any intention of ever being one ... *(aside)* clearly I'm not equipped with the huge bank of comic remarks you need to get into the police force! And before you ask ... no, I don't drink and drive.
Andy & Jazz:	*(To audience)* That's dangerous!
Andy:	I completely disapprove of such behaviour. As a young child I was a devout fan of Tufty Fluffytail. I was shocked by the repeated wrongdoing of Willy Weasel. *(Beginning to use his car as a platform for what becomes a mock political speech)* I have now come of age. I have grown up to believe, firmly, that all who commit motoring offences should be boiled alive or made to appear in Noel's House Party ... Yes you may call that harsh ... indeed cruel ... but that's how I feel about scoundrels who fail to obey the laws laid down by the *(Jazz and Andy stand and salute)* mighty Highway Code. Now, how can I help you Officer?
Police 1 & 2:	*(Completely bowled over by the speech)* It's just that you seemed to be in a bit of a hurry?
Andy:	So did you Officer ...
Jazz:	(Seductively.) And recognising that fact my partner attempted to manoeuvre his vehicle out of your, more important path.

Police 1 & 2:	*(They look at one another)* Well ... how considerate ... We must have been mis-reading our ... our little device ... well, just remember that next time ...
Jazz:	Oh ... *(Smiling broadly and confidently)* there's no possibility of there being "next time" Officer. Is there, Andy?
Andy	Indeed not!
Police 1 & 2:	There's a good boy. Then we'll leave it at that then shall we? An official warning. *(They exit)*
Andy & Jazz:	*(To audience)* What? They're letting me off! *(Look at one another in surprise, clapping hands.)* Whoa! Excellent! *(To A, adopting the accent and mannerisms of Bill & Ted)* Most triumphant! *(Guitar lick mime!)*
A:	Enough! A change of pace should be injected. Higher Education: Part One: Accepted or rejected. The season for Uni. interviews has arrived and gone And well and truly on ... Is the waiting game for Jazz and Andy Each letter on their doormat is scoured with eagle eyes *(A gives an envelope to each of them.)* Until one day the envelope arrives Containing their surprise.
Jazz:	*(Opening the envelopes)* Bretton Hall. Drama. Just what I wanted! Three D's. Amazing!
Andy:	University of York: Computer Studies. A 'B' and two 'C's. Piece of piss! I thought they'd want all B's!
Jazz & Andy:	*(To each other simultaneously)* Did you get an offer? Yeh. Where? (Bretton Hall.) (York.) Yeah!!!! Celebrate!

Section 1

A:	Hit the town and paint it red Then off to the garden shed ...
Jazz & Andy:	... for a bit of hanky panky!
A:	Part two: Which comes first, partner or Higher Ed.? *(Jazz is working on an essay. Andy is sitting, waiting for her to finish flicking through a magazine.)*
Andy:	*(Hesitantly)* Jazz? D'ya fancy going to the fair tonight?
Jazz:	I've got to do this essay for Friday morning.
Andy:	You're the only one who works this late in these study rooms. Everyone else has gone home ... or out!
Jazz:	And?
Andy:	There's always something.
Jazz:	No. Not always.
Andy:	There is ... rehearsals, and "Oh I'm sorry I've got a hair appointment."You have more hair appointments than the bloody hairdresser!
Jazz:	I never make a fuss when you've got something to do.
Andy:	Like what?
Jazz:	Work!
Andy:	That's different! I can't choose my hours there.
Jazz:	And I can't choose when to give this essay in. I've left it until the last minute as it is.
Andy:	You've got two nights!
Jazz:	And I need both of them!
Andy:	No-one bothers if it's late anyway.

24

Jazz:	Andy, listen up. I need to pass my exams. You seem to do your college work, have a job, and have loads of free time. It's not like that for me. Life's not a "piece of piss"! *(Pause)* We'll go out at the weekend ... half eight *(pointedly)* when you finish work ... and if you want to go to the fair, well go with your mates.
Andy:	I haven't been out with them since I've been going out with you.
Jazz:	That's not my fault!
Andy:	Didn't say it was.
Jazz:	*(Packs her things away)* I'm off home ... so I can concentrate!
Andy:	Let me give you a lift?
Jazz:	No.
Andy:	Why not?
Jazz:	I want to walk.
Andy:	In the rain?
Jazz:	I like the rain!
Andy:	Liar!
Jazz:	Alright ... alright ... I'll have a lift if ...
Andy:	Yes?
Jazz:	*(Bringing out a CD from her bag)* If you'll play this on your flash CD multiplay.
Andy:	What is it?
Jazz:	*(It could actually be anything ... that gets a laugh)* ?????
Andy:	You brought that to college with you! You sad person.

Section 1

Jazz:	And ...
Andy:	And?
Jazz:	And I want you to sing along.
Andy:	That's cool ... No problem!
	(The chosen song is played with Andy singing heartily ... dancing with Jazz. Aim to liven things up and raise a smile!)
A:	Part 3: A' Level results: *(Giving an envelope to each of them)*
Jazz:	Andy!
Andy:	What?
Jazz:	I've got a B and two C's!
Andy:	*(Trying hard to be pleased for her.)* You deserve them. What did your dad say?
Jazz:	He's offered to pay for my driving lessons!
Andy:	I thought you didn't want to learn to drive.
Jazz:	I didn't want you to teach me ... there's a difference!
Andy:	Frightened you might pick up my bad habits?
Jazz:	Frightened I wouldn't pick up any good ones! Well, what about yours?
Andy:	You don't want to know.
Jazz:	What do you mean?
Andy:	An A, an E and an N.
Jazz:	You're messing around!
Andy:	*(He shows her the slip of paper.)* A in Computer Studies, E in Maths and N in Chemistry.
Jazz:	You'll get in through clearing though won't you?

Andy:	Don't know if I want to anymore.
Jazz:	What are you going to do?
Andy:	I'm going for this job selling advertising space on the Net ... The guy sounded very interested in me and told me that I'll get a company car ... I'll keep the Cabriolet, for weekends ... cool eh? ... then I'll find somewhere to rent. It'll be smart.
Jazz:	What's the catch?
Andy:	There isn't one! *(Jazz's reaction lets him know she is suspicious)* Seriously ... I may even get my own laptop! Come on ... Let's go and celebrate. Everyone else's going to the Rose and Crown.
Jazz:	It wouldn't be right. Don't you care about your results?
Andy:	I want a job. I want the readies. The only thing that would have bothered me is you going off to Yorkshire and me being stuck down here with nothing to do ... but now with this ...
Jazz:	You haven't even got this job yet.
Andy:	Haven't even applied for it!
Jazz:	Well then?
Andy:	Piece of piss!
A:	Part 4: Farewell my Lovely. "Good-bye" or "Au-revoir"? The soppy bit! *(Emotional slow dance music begins.)*
Andy:	Are you nervous?
Jazz:	What do you mean?
Andy:	College ... tomorrow ... are you nervous about going?
Jazz:	You know I am! I want to go but ...

Section 1

Andy:	You'll miss me?
Jazz:	Might! *(Looking up and seeing his reaction)* I'm going to miss you a lot.
Andy:	I've dreaded this for weeks ... I can't help it but I'm frightened I'm going to lose you!
Jazz:	Why?
Andy:	It's obvious isn't it?
Jazz:	You've got just as much chance of ...
Andy:	Yeh, but I don't want to.
Jazz:	And I do?
Andy:	*(Andy shrugs his shoulders)* All I know is that the last year and a half has been amazing ...
A:	*(A walks over to Andy and gives him a sports bag.)* Absence makes the heart grow fonder ... and all that stuff?
Andy:	Jazz. *(He puts his hand inside the sports bag.)* I've got something for you. *(He brings out a giant teddy.)*
Jazz:	Andy. *(Looking at the teddy.)* He's ...
Andy:	I thought he'd remind you of me.
Jazz:	*(Holding it out to examine it)* I see the resemblance. *(They laugh.)*
Andy:	He's the one I won at Bognor.
Jazz:	He's gorgeous *(Hugs the teddy bear close to her.)*
A:	A few tearstained moments later and *(Singing as they part with Jazz waving the teddy's arm)* Andy and Teddy are waving good-bye.

Section 2:   Apart

(Possibly pre-recorded music. Matt walks over to Jazz. They drink and chat. Once this is established the focus shifts to Andy who is writing/ reading through a letter.)

Andy:	*(Writing or reading through his letter.)* Dear Jazz. I hope you're getting on OK and haven't met too many blokes you fancy! Lots to tell you. I've found a little bedsit. It'll be brilliant when you come and stay.
	(Continues to write/read (silently) as the scene continues.)
Matt:	*(Laughing)* Go on then!
Jazz:	Why?
Matt:	Just do it! Lick your palm.
Jazz:	It's a trick isn't it?
Matt:	Just do it.
Jazz:	*(Jazz licks her palm)* Now what?
Matt:	Does it taste of salt?
Jazz:	No.
Matt:	That's all right then.
Jazz:	What do you mean?
Matt:	If your palm tastes of salt it means you're going to die at sea. I heard it on the radio. Here, did you hear about the Oyster who went to the Freshers Ball?
Jazz:	No?
Matt:	He left early because he pulled a mussel!!!
Jazz:	*(Laughing)* You're mad you are!
Andy:	The people who rented this place before got chucked out and left it in a tip. The landlord made me clear it up for a discount on the first month's

	rent. The loo was disgusting with crap up the wall! Mum and dad have been incredibly helpful, although having said that I know they wish I'd found somewhere a little less basic!
Matt:	*(Jazz and Matt are laughing together.)* If you want to do a dog bark the secret is to breathe in as you do it ... like this. *(Matt impersonates a dog barking.)* Go on you try!
Jazz:	Are all footballers as mad as you?
Matt:	Barking's my little trademark ... whenever I score the whole crowd barks.
Jazz:	Seriously?
Matt:	Seriously ... so if you want to come and see me you've got to learn how to do it.
Jazz:	I don't know why I'm doing this! *(She clears her throat and makes an attempt at it. It makes her cough)*
Matt:	By Christmas ... I'll have you howling for me!
Jazz:	I'm not hanging round that long!
Matt:	That's what they all say!
Jazz:	There are that many are there?
Matt:	Millions! ... but you're special!
Jazz:	Even though I can't bark.
Matt:	Bark or no bark I'll be pleased if you'd share my bone!
Jazz:	... but not tonight ... I'm going to go back to my Hall with ... *(looks around)* Oh no, where's Allison gone?
Matt:	I'll see you back OK ... Grasshopper Hall, isn't it?
Jazz:	*(Slight pause)* Yeh.

Matt:	A dance before we go?
Jazz:	I thought you said you'd got training tomorrow morning.
Matt:	When you've seen me dribble you'll realise I don't need any training.
Jazz:	I presume you mean on the football pitch?
Matt:	What else?
Andy:	Prepare for a shock! The immaculate conception hit our town this week. You know William, as in son of Tory councillor Major Willard ... the year below us at school ... well ... Willie's girlfriend is pregnant! Major Willard is not a happy Major. *(Impersonation)* William Willard, you have defiled this beautiful young virgin in a manner entirely unbecoming of a member of our noble family. I'll have your nuts for garters my boy ... *(mimes picking a shotgun from off the wall)* ... now be gone ... and do not dare to darken our door again or I shall not be answerable for what I do! *(Mimes shooting the unfortunate Willie!)* ... actually it's the baby I worry about ... no doubt the poor little sod will be born with a waxed moustache!
Jazz:	*(Jazz and Matt are very cosy, speaking quietly and intimately)* When did this happen?
Matt:	Last year.
Jazz:	I'm really sorry ... I was only ... well you know...
Matt:	Up until quite recently if I'm asked about my family I'd not mention him. It's too difficult ... I get upset and people don't know what to say, but ... well, it's wrong ... it's not fair on him ... talking about him is the best way to keep him real.
Jazz:	I'm glad you've told me.

Section 2

Matt:	The bastard who ran into him was tested ... he was a known druggie ... people said he always drove in that state ... everyone knew, but no-one said anything ... until he ...
Jazz:	How old was he?
Matt:	Who, the driver or Frankie?
Jazz:	Frankie.
Matt:	Same age as me ... he wasn't my real brother ... but Mum and Iain got together soon after Dad left and they got married when I was about five so ... well we were really close, everything ... same bedroom, same class at school, same football teams, he was much better than me. We even had the same girlfriends sometimes .... I still haven't got over it.
Jazz:	What happened to the driver?
Matt:	Nothing until last month ... that made it even worse ... it took a year to go to court ... Iain and I wanted to go round and sort him out but ... well what's the point ... we just felt so useless.
Jazz:	Did he get sent down for it?
Matt:	Yeh ... but he can probably get more gear there than he can outside, and then what's to stop him from doing it again when he comes out? Is some one like that going to worry about a ban. Iain and me still put flowers at the place where he was killed ... there's not a lot else we can do ...
Andy:	I had a little shunt in the car yesterday so it's at the garage being fixed. Nothing serious and I was OK., so don't worry ... and it wasn't my fault ... well, not completely!
	This means I'll be coming up by train so I won't be there when I said. The train doesn't get into

the station until 1:06 in the morning! *(A takes the letter from Andy and ...)*

Jazz: *(... gives it to Jazz, who reads.)* I'm really looking forward to seeing you. Love ya, And.

Matt: *(Entering)* Who's that from?

Jazz: A friend.

A: Bit vague, are you hiding something Jazz?

Matt: No-one special then?

Jazz: Matt, it's my boyfriend ... from home.

Matt: Why didn't you say before?

Jazz: Too scared, I guess.

Matt: Scared?

Jazz: We've been going out for over a year.

Matt: Caroline and I have been seeing each other for eight months.

Jazz: He's coming up on Friday. I'll tell him over the weekend.

Matt: I haven't got a match on Saturday so ... we could tell them both together!

Jazz: I don't want you to tell her about me.

Matt: Why not? She'll find out eventually.

Jazz: I don't want her to say anything while he's around. I can't tell Andy on Friday ... I can't do that to him ... he's got nowhere else to go ... but I will tell him ... on Sunday morning, before he leaves.

Matt: So you're going to be with him all weekend.

Jazz: Yeh, but you mustn't worry ... I want to finish with him ... I will tell him.

Section 2

A:	*(Andy enters carrying a sports bag and studying some directions.)* Somewhere near Grasshopper Hall on Friday night Andy's lost
Andy:	*(Angrily)* Jazz's map is Shiite!
A:	Then walking towards him ... a figure he can see
Andy:	*(To Matt.)* Oy. Excuse-me. Please can you help me.
A:	What a coincidence!
Matt:	Yeh, what is it mate?
Andy:	Is this Grasshopper Hall?
Matt:	Yes.
Andy:	I'm looking for Room 102.
Matt:	102? Jazzy Maihnah?
Andy:	Yeh.
Matt:	There's a guy on duty by the lift. He'll let you in ... if she's expecting you.
Andy:	I'm her boyfriend.
Matt:	Are you mate?
Andy:	Yeh. I've just arrived up here by train.
Matt:	You ... are her boyfriend?
Andy:	Yeh. Why?
Matt:	Just that I know her! You're a lucky bloke you are. Anyway ... when you see her ... tell her Barking Matt says hello. *(Exits Barking)*
Jazz:	*(Enters)* He's just a friend Andy.
Andy:	*(Turning)* Well, why would he say that then?
Jazz:	I don't even know what he said properly.

Andy:	He just seemed surprised when I told him I was your boyfriend.
Jazz:	He was probably winding you up. Anyway he's got a girlfriend who lives in the next door Hall. That's how I met him. He doesn't even go to the college.
Andy:	What was he doing here?
Jazz:	Seeing her I suppose.
Andy:	How well do you know him?
Jazz:	Reasonably ... what is this?
Andy:	What does he do? Is he a student?
Jazz:	He's a footballer.
Andy:	Professional?
Jazz:	Yeh.
Andy:	Who does he play for?
Jazz:	Does it matter?
Andy:	I'm just curious.
Jazz:	You don't even like football, but if you must know, he plays for York.
Andy:	As in York City?
Jazz:	I suppose so.
Andy:	Ah! He's the pratt they all bark at ... bloody show off was on TV last week.
Jazz:	Andy, what are you getting so worked up about?
Andy:	Apparently the supporters all bark ... you know like a dog when he scores ... cocky git! He even barked when he walked away from me. He fancies himself. I got the impression he fancied you too.

Jazz:	Let's not talk about him any more. Don't spoil the weekend Andy or I'll wish you hadn't come.
A:	*(As though a football commentator, an imitation would be ideal)* And she reaches for ... is it a red? ... no a yellow card. Just the warning but with Matt Irvine constantly hanging around the box, Andy Bowen has to be careful.
	And there goes the final whistle, (Andy exits) Andy Bowen escapes this week as he walks back to the dressing room head down and tail firmly between his legs. But who's this? It's Matt Irvine. *(Matt enters ... all in slow motion. It is essential that Jazz and Matt are choreographed appropriately to indicate the meaning of the words.)* He's placing the ball on the spot. A very short run up and ... yes he's scored! What a goal ... and it's allowed. Just listen to the crowd barking like rabid dogs ... what a reaction! Football certainly is a funny old game and Matt Irvine has undoubtedly earned his place in this team, surely consigning poor, out of form Andy Bowen to the inevitable free transfer.
Matt:	*(To audience)* ... if anyone will have him. You'll never guess what.
Jazz:	What?
Matt:	I met your boyfriend.
Jazz:	Yes, he said.
Matt:	*(Laughing)* He asked me for directions. Me?
Jazz:	I know.
Matt:	So ... have you told him?
Jazz:	I'm going to.
Matt:	What?

Jazz:	I've arranged to go down and see him next week end. I'll tell him ... it'll be so much easier cos I can just go back home for the rest of the weekend. It was too difficult here and I felt too guilty what with him coming up all this way.
Matt:	Why can't you just do it on the phone?
Jazz:	He deserves more than that.
Matt:	What about me?
Jazz:	What do you mean?
Matt:	You sounded so definite before ... what changed your mind..
Jazz:	Nothing. Trust me.
Matt:	What ... like he does?
Andy:	*(Jazz & Matt kiss and talk closely throughout Andy's letter.)* Dear Jazz, When I got back home yesterday night I sat in my bath and cried for ages. I looked at the photos of us at Bogner and that made me even more sad. I'm seriously thinking of packing my job in and coming up to York to be with you. I'm sure I could find something. What do you think? We could find somewhere to rent together ... it'd be so excellent ...
A:	On and on the letter goes ... In Andy's rather soppy prose. A fresh one in the post each day... *(Jazz is given a bouquet. Matt is not impressed and turns away)* And then a very posh bouquet.
Jazz:	*(To Matt)* Alright! It's not my fault! I didn't ask him to send the bloody thing!

Section 3:   Fatality

A:
Wednesday afternoon ... Andy's in a flurry
Hurrying
To an appointment
Can't rub ointment
On the fact he's late
Which only serves to vindicate
To him ... his gratuitous greed ...
... for speed.

Andy:
(Spoken hurriedly, anxiously, as though "against the clock".) My organisation is always such that if I know I can do a journey in twenty minutes I'll only give it twenty minutes, I know it's stupid more so because work are very strict on time keeping. Fortunately it's a great day for driving, the weather's perfect, so I just try to make some time up.

A:
So Andy contrives a custom built cause to go quick
After all, speeding's only "speeding" if you're doing it for a kick.
The ingredients all laid out before you,
ready to inflict
The R.T.A. so painfully easy to predict ... and yet so simple ... to avoid.

Kelly:
(Wearing outdoor clothes. Preparing to go out, putting a coat and rucksack on. Calling as though upstairs where Dad/Mum is ironing.) Dad/(Mum)!

Brian (or Cath):
(Entering) What?

Kelly:
Can you lend me a fiver to get some petrol for my moped...interview at the supermarket. Remember?

Brian (or Cath):
Forgot ... sorry.

Kelly:
I'll pay you back when I get my job!

Brian (or Cath):
(Getting the money from his/her wallet)
What happens if you don't?

Kelly:
I will. He already said he liked the look of me!

Brian (or Cath): You watch him. *(S/He gives Kelly the money)*

Kelly: Thanks Dad/Mum. *(Kisses him/her. Picks up (from A?) a cheap and much used motorcycle helmet.)* I'll be back as soon as I can ... just after five I guess.

Brian (or Cath): Good luck Kelly. *(Freeze)*

Andy: *(To audience)* I've already made up some time cos I know this journey well and the roads are really clear. There's this bend coming up, round to the left, wide with verges on both sides which sweeps out into a straight, and I'm setting myself a challenge, thinking, "How fast can I go?". *(With relish)* I take the bend at about 80. You can feel the car teasing round the corner on the edge of control ... the tyres not quite screeching. Amazing!

A: Isn't there a school on one side?

Andy: *(To A, snapping "out of the previous speech")* Yeh, my old school. They finished about an hour ago ... in any case the school's all fenced off this side, so that's no problem. *(In slow motion, with the fx as used in Section 1 Andy "comes back into the scene", speaking to audience. He starts speaking once his "driving" position has been reassumed.)* I'm on the straight now and I'm decelerating cos there's a bend coming up. I guess I'm doing about 60 ...

A: *(To Audience)* More like 70.

Andy: *(To A, again snapping "out of the previous speech")* Everyone breaks the speed limit here!

A: Everyone?

Andy: Take the 40 sign away, you'd guess it's deristricted, or a 60. If they wanted to stop it they'd have police ... or ... you know, cameras there or something, in any case speed helps me to focus my mind. When I drive fast I concentrate more and I drive more carefully. Anyway, I'm on the straight now, doing 60 ... *(with a grin to A)* ... or 70, no longer feeling as if I'm going "fast".

A: *(Standing to the left of Andy)* Garage forecourt.

Kelly: *(Kelly is surrounded by three threatening individuals, B, C, & D)* Girl on moped.

A: Excellent visibility.

All *(Except Andy)*: Throttle!

Andy: She's not looking!

All *(Except Andy)*: Throttle!

All: Stop!!!

(Kelly & A-D say this to Andy. Andy to Kelly. "A" simultaneously attempts to reach out to prevent Andy from hitting Kelly. There could equally be those who attempt to "stop" Kelly.

It is important in the following moments that the elements of the crash are explored physically as the words are spoken. The violence of the death, and the pain he repeatedly and without mercy, inflicts on her should be highlighted in the physicalisation.

In slow motion the audience should be able to scrutinise the reactions of all those involved in far greater detail. Andy should actually be seen to be hurting Kelly ... beating her up either with fists or metal bars repeatedly every time she is "hit" in the accident after the initial impact. The "blows" in the written script are for guidance only ... it is the violence of the accident that should be conveyed rather than these instructions to be followed blindly.)

B: Sound the horn!

C: Steer away.

D: Slams on brakes.

All *(Except Andy)*: Wheels lock ... Skid!

B *(The witness)*: Car ... opposite direction ... swerves.

All:	(As Andy makes his first violent - slow motion - contact with Kelly) No!!!
B:	(2nd blow) Her body smashes through the windscreen.
C:	(3rd blow) Smashes against his head as he is forced forward.
D:	Rolls over the roof ...
B:	Down the back panel.
D:	Onto the grass verge.
All (Except Andy):	(Andy throws his final blow. Kelly is lowered into her "resting" position by A-D simulating her final slow motion fall.) Into a lamp post.
	(Silence)
Andy:	I come to a halt on the grass verge ... glass everywhere. (Re-living the crash) I can't stop seeing that face ... frozen in horror as I skid towards it then turning back, trying to carry on. I hit the bike on the right hand side of the road, if I hadn't have swerved ... if I'd've carried on straight, I'd've missed it altogether.
	I get out of the car ... I turn round to see what has happened, and there's a mangled body slumped by the lamp-post.
	People come over from the houses.
Neighbour 1:	(Attending to girl) Someone get an ambulance ... Quick!
Neighbour 2:	It's a young girl ... anyone know any First Aid?
Andy:	"Is she still breathing?"
Neighbour 1:	It's shallow.
Andy:	She's still alive then? She didn't look ... she just flew out of the garage.

Section 3

Neighbour 3:	Come on mate. You've got a lot of cuts on your face.
Andy:	It's nothing serious.
Neighbour 3:	*(Moving Andy away from Kelly.)* Let's get you over here and wait for the ambulance.
Andy:	*(To Audience.)* I can see the bone in her leg sticking out, just like raw meat on a butcher's table. I'm thinking, "It didn't matter what speed I was going. I still wouldn't've had time to stop. *(Grabbing and addressing Neighbour 2)* Agree with me! Agree with me! Please, tell me there was nothing I could do! Tell me she didn't look! *(Pause)* Tell me you don't think I was going too fast!
Neighbour 3:	*(Trying to calm Andy)* No-one's doubting you mate and you've got a witness. The woman in the other car must have seen what happened.
Andy:	*(Slowly)* Yes ... yes I suppose she must have done. *(To audience)* The police and the ambulance arrived very quickly, about 7 or 8 minutes I suppose.
Paramedic 1:	*(Entering)* Look at the skid marks. 100 metres I reckon.
Paramedic 2:	He must have been doing some.
Paramedic 1:	Smashed the helmet ... another cheap one.
Paramedic 2:	Ankle torn away ... and the two bones below her knee are out. *(Paramedic 3 enters and goes over to Andy)*
Paramedic 1:	Blood from the ear and nose ... Suspect a severe injury to the base of her skull ... or depressed fractures.
	(They continue the examination and load Kelly in to a stretcher and take her off during the following dialogue.)
Paramedic 3:	What's your name?

Andy:	Andy. Andy Bowen.
Paramedic:	Right Andy. I've come over to see how you are. Do you think you've got any injuries?
Andy:	No. Look don't you think you'd be more use over there.
Paramedic:	I've come to check you over. It's important we check you over too, and then the police'll want to breathalyse you.
Andy:	There's no need to worry about that ... I don't drink and drive. *(Andy is being checked throughout the remaining conversation.)* The girl on the moped ... they say her breathing's very shallow.
Paramedic:	She's quite seriously injured.
Andy:	Is she going to die?
Paramedic:	I can't really say that at this point. They're doing all they can for her.
Andy:	What if she does?
Paramedic:	You can't think like that. Just be thankful you're not badly injured ... as far as I can see, you've only got minor grazes to your face. It could have been much worse.
Andy:	Yeh. I could have been her.
Paramedic:	*(Paramedic completes his checks. There is a moment of silence.)* Right Andy. I need to go and tell the police that you're ready to see them now.
Andy:	How old is she? Do you know?
Paramedic:	She had "L" plates. I doubt she was a very experienced driver.
Andy:	What do you reckon? Sixteen?

Paramedic:	Maybe. It's hard to say. *(Silence)* It's not going to be easy, you do realise that, don't you?
Witness:	*(Approaching paramedic out of Andy's earshot.)* The man driving that car was driving like a maniac ... he was going ... I don't know how fast he was going ... I saw it all ... I just need to tell someone ... that poor motorcyclist ... she didn't stand a chance.
Brian (or Cath):	Once the moped started across the road he appears ... 100 metres away.
Andy:	*(To audience)* The police tell me that the girl's name is Kelly and that she's sixteen years old.
Brian (or Cath):	Travelling at over seventy in a forty.
Andy:	*(To audience)* I tell the police that as far as I know I wasn't exceeding the speed limit.
Brian (or Cath):	You gave Kelly one and a half seconds to turn back ...
All except Andy:	... there was nothing she could have done.
Andy:	She came out without looking. There was nothing I could do!
Brian (or Cath):	Then they allowed you to go home. *(B, C, D & Kelly leave inconspicuously.)*
Andy:	I phone a couple of people and have a few drinks. I imagine the doorstep scene for Kelly's parents and I feel guilty ... bloody guilty. I imagine them crying at her bedside ... this poor mangled kid. I ring the hospital and enquire about Kelly's condition but they won't tell me anything. I am so angry ... really frustrated. "You've got to tell me! Tell me! I'm the driver of the car who crashed into her. Why won't you tell me?" But they won't. Then

the phone rings:

D.I. Morris:	Is that Mr. Andrew Bowen?
Andy:	Yes.
Brian (or Cath):	What's happened?
D.I. Morris:	This is Inspector Morris. Mr. Bowen I'm afraid I have some very bad news to tell you regarding your accident yesterday afternoon.
Andy:	She's died hasn't she?
Brian (or Cath):	No ... killed! Brutally killed by some maniac driver. They say he was doing at least 70 miles an hour ... 70 in a forty! ... what chance did she stand?
D.I. Morris:	Do you have a solicitor?
Andy:	I know one, but, well, I don't think I'd use him. *(He puts the phone down slowly)*
Brian (or Cath):	*(Suddenly to Andy encircling him)* Let the courts deal with it?! ... they won't do nothing ... No, you come over and see us ... our friends. Walk up our path ... into our front room and pack away her things for us ... the CD she was playing before she left for that interview ... her ... and ... *(Pause)* ... what are we going to do with her room?

(Pause)

What am I going to do with her room?

Section 4:   Outcast

A: Both Andy and Jazz have something to tell
            The memory of which they'll find hard to expel
            She to admit concealing the truth
            And he to confess dealing death to a youth.

            *(Andy, carrying sports bag in one hand, has just
            arrived in Jazz's room where a tape plays quietly
            throughout scene.)*

Andy: Jazz, Am I glad to see you? *(Goes to hug her)*

Jazz: *(Holding him at arms length and looking at his cut
            face)* Andy, what have you been doing? These cuts?
            (Concerned) Have you been involved in a fight?

Andy: No ... well, not yet anyway.

Jazz: What do you mean?

Andy: *(Moving away from her, goes down on his knees
            to unzip his bag and takes out a bottle of wine)*
            Have you got a corkscrew?

Jazz: I don't know. *(Half-heartedly looks for a corkscrew)*

Andy: Can't you ask one of your friends?

Jazz: *(Taking the wine.)* I don't want to drink *(Putting the
            wine back in Andy's bag)* and I don't want you
            drinking either.

Andy: Why not?

Jazz: When you phoned this afternoon I dropped my
            plans for tonight so that I could see you. Something
            must be wrong! If you've got something to say,
            please, say it to me while you're sober.

Andy: I just thought it would help to bring a bottle of wine.

Jazz: And if you're not going to say anything ... well,
            there are things I need to tell you.

Andy:	Jazz ... I'm in trouble. Big trouble. *(Pause. Then without emotion)* I've killed someone.
Jazz:	*(Long pause)* What?
Andy:	A sixteen year old girl, Kelly McFarlane. She was on a moped and I ran into her.
Jazz:	When?
Andy:	Wednesday afternoon.
Jazz:	Where?
Andy:	Burbury Road.
Jazz:	Behind our old school?
Andy:	She just came out of the garage without looking.
Jazz:	And you weren't injured?
Andy:	Cuts from the windscreen.
Jazz:	Maybe we will open that bottle of wine. *(Moving to leave the room.)* I'll go and get a corkscrew.
Andy:	They say I was speeding.
Jazz:	*(Jazz stops 'in her tracks' and turns slowly)* Were you?
Andy:	I don't know.
Jazz:	Weren't there any witnesses?
Andy:	One.
Jazz:	And?
Andy:	It doesn't really matter any more.
Jazz:	What do you mean?
Andy:	They reckon I was well over the speed limit.
Jazz:	Who?

Andy:	The Accident Investigation Unit. They made me sit and watch them do these tests. They wanted me to break down and admit it. It was terrifying, watching this police car driving along at forty, and then braking at the point in the road where my skid marks began. It stopped a good fifty metres from the garage. They kept on, getting faster and faster. Eventually, at just over seventy, the car skidded right up to where I hit the moped.
Jazz:	*(Quietly disbelieving)* Seventy?
Andy:	Everybody drives fast along there.
Jazz:	Not that fast!
	(Silence)
Andy:	They're probably going to charge me ...
Jazz:	What with?
Andy:	... I'm going to fight it. Death by Dangerous Driving. If I'd been pulled up by the police before it happened, I'd've been done for speeding, not dangerous driving ... it only became dangerous when she pulled out without looking. She was a learner.
Jazz:	*(Suddenly more detached)* Andy, how did you get up here?
Andy:	What?
Jazz:	Did you come by train? Please tell me you came by train.
Andy:	I drove.
Jazz:	You what?
Andy:	There's nothing illegal about it! They can't ban me until it goes to court. *(Silence. Jazz turns her back*

on Andy.) If you're going to be like that, maybe I should go. *(Zips up bag)* Maybe I should drive back now. Is that what you want? *(Andy turns to leave. Jazz does not respond. She remains motionless, facing away from him. Long Pause. Slowly Andy turns to face Jazz's back)* Jazz, you're all I've got. I need you to help me. *(Andy approaches Jazz. Slowly, she turns to face him still at some distance.)*

Jazz: *(Pause)* When does it go to court?

Andy: Anything from six to eighteen months.

Jazz: What'll you get?

Andy: A long ban, a huge bloody fine ... I don't know where I'll get the money from and I'll probably have to pack my job in. There's already been an article in the evening paper back home making me out to be some kind of a mass murderer. I need to get away. But I've had an idea. That's why I wanted to see you! How about if I came and lived up here ... with you ... where nobody knows ... Please Jazz ... please! There's nothing else I can do!

Jazz: Andy ... I ... It's not a simple as that.

Andy: Why Jazz? Please ... please? *(Andy holds out his arms.Both he and Jazz are motionless for a moment or two ... Jazz not sure how she should react. Finally she moves towards him ... he moves to hug her. She responds with reservations)*

Jazz: *(Hugging)* Come on Andy. Come on. *(The sound of someone "barking" repeatedly and loudly off stage)*

Andy: What the hell's that?

Jazz: *(Under her breath)* Shit!

Matt: *(Enters. Stops as he sees Andy & Jazz. Jazz separates herself from Andy and moves away.)* Bad timing eh? At least this explains why you weren't at the match!

Jazz: I didn't know Andy was coming until ... well he phoned me at ...

Andy: What match?

Matt: Crystal Palace at home in the Cup mate!

Andy: *(To Jazz)* So that's what you had to cancel then?

Matt: We won three-one. I scored two. The first was an overhead kick, I've never done that before, in a professional game ... and there was this scout there from Man U.

Jazz: I tried to phone but you weren't in and the club was engaged.

Matt: I really thought you'd seen it. All our lot were barking really loud ... it was brilliant ... really funny ... I was dead chuffed. I mean you said you'd be there. I waited around afterwards but ... well, you didn't show. I felt such a pratt.

Andy: Am I hearing this right?

Matt: I told all my mates you were coming down. I wanted them to meet you.

Andy: Jazz, what the hell's going on?

Jazz: It's a bit complicated.

Andy: Complicated?

Matt: It never crossed your mind that I'd come over after the match did it?

Jazz: Matt, something's happened!

Andy: *(Becoming angry, and raising his voice)* You promised me last week everything was OK.

Jazz:	Andy! Keep the noise down or ...
Andy:	No ... why should I? Have you been seeing him, or something? *(Jazz does not answer. Pause. To Matt.)* I mean what else am I to think?
Matt:	I'd say you're getting pretty warm mate ...
Andy:	And I'd say you're trying to wind me up! *(Andy confronts Matt. Jazz gets between them.)*
Matt:	So, what are you going to do ... take a pop at me? That'd really impress her wouldn't it?
Andy:	It'd make me feel better.
Matt:	Come on then! It'll go down a storm in the tabloids! "Two Goal Cup Hero, Irvine ... Beaten up in College Brawl".
Jazz:	Matt, stop it!
Andy:	Why didn't you tell me?
Jazz:	I was going to but ... well, I couldn't ... not after ... *(To Matt)* Look, Andy's been involved in a car crash.
	(Silence)
Matt:	He seems alright.
Andy:	I killed a sixteen year old kid ... she was on a moped and I ran into her.
Matt:	You what?
Andy:	That's not all! The girl's family trying to nail me with her death ... saying it was my fault ...
Matt:	And? Was it?
Andy:	No! She pulled out without looking ...
Matt:	They wouldn't try to blame you if there weren't a good reason for it.

Section 4

Andy:	What do you know about it?
Matt:	What was it? Drunk driving? Speeding? Overtaking on a blind bend?
Andy:	She pulled out without looking.
Matt:	So why didn't you stop?
Andy:	There wasn't time! What is this?
Matt:	What do her family say you were doing?
Andy:	You're mad!
Jazz:	He was driving too fast ...
Matt:	How fast? I want to know how fast you were going?
Andy:	I don't have to tell you anything. It was an accident!
Matt:	*(Approaching and grabbing Andy overpowering him)* You don't drive too fast by "accident". You chose to put your foot on the accelerator ... no-one made you do it! How fast were you going?
Jazz:	Tell him Andy.
Andy:	*(To Jazz)* Tell him to let go of me! *(Matt twists Andy's arm provoking the response)*
Jazz:	Seventy.
Matt:	And the speed limit?
Andy:	She's told you so let go. *(Matt puts more pressure on Andy ... he squeals)*
Jazz:	Forty ... Matt! Let go of him or I'll get the warden.
Matt:	*(He throws Andy away.)* Seventy ... in a forty. Why?
Andy:	What do you mean "why"?
Matt:	There must've been a reason.

Andy: Everyone drives fast along that road ...

Matt: No wonder the family are gunning for you.

Andy: I'm a victim too!

Matt: You're sick!

Andy: She's really making me suffer ... Kelly bloody MacFarlane.

Jazz: Andy don't.

Matt: She suffered more than you can ever know ... and her family.

Andy: You've no right to stand in judgement over me ... not after what you've done!

Matt: pretty   Getting off with your girlfriend, who gave me a clear "come on", ain't in the same league as killing someone mate.

Jazz: *(To Matt)* I think you should go now.

Matt: *(To Jazz)* Maybe I should ... before I do something I might really regret.

Jazz: Just go.

Matt: *(To Andy)* I lost my brother because of some maniac driver! I wasn't allowed to go in and say good-bye to him, because his body was so badly torn apart. And then you talk about being a victim. I never had the guts to do anything about it, although I really wanted to beat the hell out of that guy. And now ... face to face with you and there's still nothing I can do!

     I hope you do time ... cos you really need to ... *(To Jazz as he turns to leave)* Maybe I'll call you tomorrow Jazz. *(Matt exits.)*

     (Long silence)

Andy:	He's got me all wrong. I do care about what I've done. I am sorry! It's just that I don't think it was all my fault ... that's all I was trying to say. You've got to believe me Jazz.
	(Long awkward silence)
Jazz:	I didn't want it to be like this.
Andy:	I bet you didn't.
	(Pause)
Jazz:	I can't talk you into staying?
Andy:	Then what? *(Gets the wine out of his bag and puts it on the table as he rants.)* Have a party? Get a take-away? Down the wine together? *(Moves over to her and grabs her threateningly).* Pretend Matt doesn't exist and make mad passionate love? *(Throws her onto the bed. Silence)* I don't think so. There's no reason to stay ... no reason to prolong the agony.
Jazz:	You're in no fit state to drive.
Andy:	I don't care. Nothing I do now can make matters any worse.
Jazz:	If there's one thing you could do for her family it'd be to stop driving.
Andy:	What do you know about it?
Jazz:	I listened to what Matt said! Anyway, you should know! Don't you remember how you felt when your Grandad died?
Andy:	What's that got to do with it?
Jazz:	The court case is ... what ... next month?
Andy:	So?

Jazz:	What do you want to happen to those kids?
Andy:	You know ...
Jazz:	You want them locked up! You want the key thrown away. I can hear you saying it!
Andy:	He was a defenceless old man. They were robbing him! They were breaking the law!
Jazz:	And she was a defenceless young girl ... this Kelly ... and you were breaking the law! What could she have done with you going at seventy miles an hour into her.
Andy:	That's not fair Jazz. They were criminals.
Jazz:	What you've done is criminal!
Andy:	Not in the same way!
Jazz:	You've taken someone's life. You kill someone and the next minute you're out driving around in your car!
Andy:	*(Andy makes to exit)* You don't know anything!
Jazz:	Where are you going?
Andy:	Haven't got a clue! *(He exits)*
Jazz:	Andy ...
A:	And so On that sour note Jazz and Andy go Each their separate way But this play Is not done till one year on ... Crown Court judgement day.
All:	How do you plead?
Andy:	Not guilty.
Cath/Brian:	You drove right into her.

Section 4

Prosecutor:	Once she started across the road you appear one hundred metres away ...
Cath/Brian:	Travelling at seventy in a Forty.
Prosecutor:	You gave her one and a half seconds to turn back.
Andy:	She pulled out without looking.
Cath/Brian:	There was nothing she could do!
Andy:	She pulled out without looking.
Cath/Brian:	Your speed was inexcusable.
Andy:	I admit I was speeding!
Cath/Brian:	No-one in their right mind drives down that road at that speed!
Prosecutor:	Why can't you admit you killed her?
Judge:	"Human blood is heavy; the man that has shed it cannot run away."
	(Silence)
A:	A verdict of "Guilty!" is quickly returned Our "hero" begins to feel somewhat spurned Still confident the sentence won't be strong Soon to realise ... he was wrong. They strip away his freedom ... tear away his pride. He's given ...
All:	... eighteen months ...
A:	... banged up inside.
Andy:	... but it was a car accident.
All:	And a five year driving ban.
	(Silence. Everyone exits leaving Andy alone on stage.)

Andy: The shock and distress of killing someone is immense, I wouldn't want to understate it at all ... but the shock and life upset of going to prison is even greater. It's a sad fact but true. Drivers don't realise, that if someone steps out in front of you and you happen to be over the speed limit ... you could end up in prison.

Prisoner 1: So you're the one who killed a sixteen year old kid!

Andy: It was a car accident.

Prisoner 2: You're smiling!

Andy: I'm just nervous.

Prisoner 1: You're laughing about it.

Andy: I'm trying to put a brave face on it.

Prisoner 2: You're not taking it very seriously!

Andy: It's my first time in prison.

Prisoner 1: Yeh, and everyone knows you didn't even have the bottle to plead guilty.

Andy: That's not true!

Prisoner 2: Why didn't you admit it then?

Andy: It wasn't all my fault.

Prisoner 1: You're not listening!

Andy: Me ... What about you?

Prisoner 2: You're not even sorry!

Andy: Let me explain!

Prisoner 1: You killed a kid. What is there to explain?

Andy: These massive blokes burst into my cell and one brought out a jug from behind his back, full of

boiling water, and hurled it at me ... in my face ...
everywhere. Then they ran out, banging the cell
door locked behind them.

The boiling water was laced with sugar ... which
made it stick to my skin ... lethal! Fortunately I had
a sink, so I put the plug in, switched on the cold
water, and plunged my face straight in. Although
that helped I couldn't stop it soaking through my
sweatshirt and leaving painful red marks on my
chest that'll no doubt serve as a reminder for the
rest of my life.

*(In slow motion Prisoners each hurl the contents of a (mimed) jug at
Andy, who screams a prolonged scream. The style of the final moment of
action should reflect elements of the staging of the accident scene in
Section 3, i.e. "an eye for an eye". The lights cross fade and remain on
the slogan at the back of the stage.)*

If you have enjoyed reading and/or working with this playscript, you may like to find out about other plays by Mark Wheeller. There are brief descriptions and other details on the following pages.

All plays are suitable for Youth Theatres, Schools, Colleges, and adult AmDram. They are ideal for GCSE Drama/English exam use and frequently do well in One Act Play Festivals. They offer both male and female performers with equally challenging opportunities.

All enquiries regarding performing rights should be made to:
Meg Davis, MBA Literary Agents, 62 Grafton Way, London W1P 5LD.
Tel: 020 7387 2076
E-mail: meg@mbalit.co.uk

For enquiries or to order plays published by *dbda*, please contact:
Bharti Bhikha or Manna Tailor, *dbda*, Pin Point, Rosslyn Crescent, Harrow HA1 2SB.
Tel: 0870 333 7771
Fax: 0870 333 7772
Email: info@dbda.co.uk

For Mark's other plays, please see details on the last page.

Other Plays by Mark Wheeller published by *dbda*

Mark Wheeller

Too Much Punch for Judy

Cast: 2m & 2f with doubling, or 3f, 3m & 6   *Duration:* 35 minutes
KS 4 to adult

A hard-hitting documentary play, based on a tragic drink-drive accident that results in the death of Jo, front seat passenger. The driver, her sister Judy, escapes unhurt (or has she?). This play has become one of the most frequently performed plays ever!

'The play will have an impact on young people or adults. It will provoke discussion. It stimulates and wants you to cry out for immediate social action and resolution.'

Henry Shankula - Addiction Research Foundation, Toronto

ISBN 1 902843 05 3   **Price: £ 5.50 per book / £70.00 for a set of 15**

Mark Wheeller

Why did the chicken cross the road?

(Because some stupid turkey egged her on!!)

Cast: 2m & 2f with doubling, or 3f, 3m & 3   *Duration:* 35 minutes
KS 3 & 4

The story of two cousins, Tammy and Chris. Tammy gets killed in a stupid game of 'Chicken' on the one morning that the cousins do not cycle to school. Chris, unable to tell anyone else about his part in the accident, has to live with this dreadful secret.

'An imaginative and moving look at risk taking at a time when peer pressure is at its strongest.

Rosie Welch, LARSOA

ISBN 1 902843 00 2   **Price: £ 4.95 per book / £65.00 for a set of 15**

Mark Wheeller

Hard to Swallow

Adapted from "Catherine" by Maureen Dunbar

Cast: 3f & 2m with doubling, or 6f, 3m & 16   *Duration:* 70 minutes
KS 3 to adult

This play is an adaptation of Maureen Dunbar's award winning book (and film) **Catherine** which charts her daughter's uneven battle with Anorexia and the family's difficulties in coping with the illness.

'This play reaches moments of almost unbearable intensity... naturalistic scenes flow seamlessly into sequences of highly stylised theatre... such potent theatre!'

Vera Lustiq - The Independent

ISBN 1 902843 08 8   **Price: £ 5.50 per book / £70.00 for a set of 15**

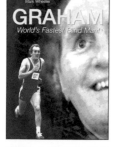

Mark Wheeller

GRAHAM
World's Fastest Blind Man

Cast: 5m & 4f with doubling, or up to 34   *Duration:* 80 minutes
KS 3/4 to adult

A play full of lively humour telling the story of **Graham Salmon MBE**. Totally blind since birth, Graham went on to become the World's Fastest Blind Man running 100 metres in 11.4 seconds!

'I was really wowed by "Graham"... offered excellent opportunities for imaginative stylised performance with GCSE students... The peaks of tension and moments of pathos really moved me... I will definitely be offering "Graham" to my classes this year.'

Neil Phillips, Head of Drama and Edexcel GCSE Examiner

ISBN 1 902843 09 6   **Price: £ 5.50 per book / £70.00 for a set of 15**

Wacky Soap - a 'gutsy' Musical to entertain and make them think...

Wacky Soap is a Pythonesque allegorical tale about drug abuse (also applies to alcohol or tobacco). While washing with Wacky Soap leads to instant happiness and an inclination towards outrageous behaviour, prolonged use washes away limbs and ultimately leads to dematerialisation. This has become a tried and tested (and increasingly popular) School/ Drama Club/Youth Theatre production and is an ideal vehicle for a cast of any age.

'This (play) gave every member of the large and energetic cast opportunities to shine... King Huff addressed his subjects from a Bouncy Castle, just one of the touches of visual humour in this fast, funny and thought provoking evening'.

Barbara Hart, Southern Evening Echo, Curtain Call Nominated "Best Production 2000"

ISBN 1 902843 02 9

KS 3/4 to adult
Duration: *50 mins play / 80 mins musical*
Cast: *6-100!*

Includes follow-up work for KS 3/4.

Price:
£ 4.95 per book / £65.00 for a set of 15

ISBN 1 902843 06 1

A companion book containing the **Music Score** *for all songs in the play and a* **Mini-Musical** *version for Junior Schools.*

KS 3 & 4
Duration: *40 mins*

Price:
£ 4.95 per book / £65.00 for a set of 15

A past performance CD gives you the opportunity to hear the songs of the play.

Price:
£15.00 each

Also available is a fully orchestrated backing track CD.

Price:
£25.00 each

ISBN 1 902843 07 X

A fully illustrated book with the story of Wacky Soap in narrative form. It serves as an ideal (and quick) way of intro-ducing the scheme of work, included in the full script.

Price:
£ 6.95 per book / £90.00 for a set of 15

Dear Mark,
'Wacky Soap' was an outstanding success!!! We had a great deal of fun doing the show and we're still laughing... to quote our Head Teacher... 'the best school show I have ever seen'. We have had letters from people in the audience saying what a fab show it was and how impressed they were. The most frequent comment was that it was a 'risk' to put it on as a school show (as opposed to doing 'Oliver' or 'Little Shop of Horrors') and one that thoroughly paid off!! 'The feel good factor was amazing' was another comment we had. Many people said how impressed they were by the 'community' spirit of the production - everybody working together without the 'star' element creeping in! So thank you - it has given us a huge boost!!

John Plant, Head of Drama, Southmoor School, Sunderland

Mark Wheeller's

GRAHAM
World's Fastest Blind Runner!

A play telling the amazing true life story of World Champion Blind Athlete Graham Salmon MBE who sadly died in 1999. It was premiered at the 2002 Edinburgh Festival Fringe.

"I came to know Graham Salmon in 1982 when, with Epping Youth Theatre, I wrote a play telling about his inspiring life. We became close friends. In 1998 Graham suffered an unbelievably cruel twist of fate. A malignant tumour was discovered in his leg...it had to be amputated.

Shortly afterwards my seven year old son, Charlie, asked Graham if he would join him in a game of football. I was concerned by this request but Graham had no such worries and took Charlie outside and played football with him... taking shots with his remaining leg and, as he became tired, used his crutch and did some headers!

It is for me the most "personal" play I think I shall ever write. Graham's life story is actually full of humour. The role of Graham provides an excellent opportunity for any actor. Most of my plays have been performed (brilliantly) by young people, adults in amateur companies and professional actors. I hope that GRAHAM will be embraced with equal enthusiasm."

Mark Wheeller

"Graham Salmon is the most inspiring athlete I have met; I say this without a moments hesitation even though I have enjoyed the rare privilege of sharing the company of Muhammad Ali, Stanley Matthews, Gary Sobers, Martina Navratilova, Nadia Comaneci, Arnold Palmer and countless others in the course of my job."

Robert Philip, Daily Telegraph

"A remarkable play ... a story of great courage and dedication; It is also entertaining and good theatre, with plenty of scope for imaginative direction."

Amateur Stage Book Review
(of the original Race To Be Seen)

Available from:

dbda, Pin Point, Rosslyn Crescent, Harrow HA1 2SB.
Tel: 0870 333 7771   Fax: 0870 333 7772   Email: info@dbda.co.uk

New for 2003: 'Dan Nolan - Missing'

by Mark Wheeller

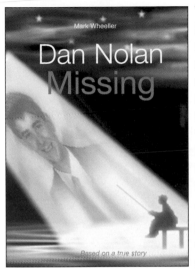

This is based on the true story of Dan Nolan, a teenage boy who went missing on 1st January 2002. The play, written in the same documentary style as 'Too Much Punch for Judy' uses the words of Daniel's family, friends (and for the first time, those who were with him that night) and the Detective in charge of the ongoing investigation, to try and get as close to the truth as memory will allow.

The play opens up some important issues relating to personal safety and will, we are sure, become a much used and thought provoking play in schools.

Like Mark's other plays, it is ideal as a GCSE or 'A' level text and Youth Theatre, Upper School, Sixth Form, Higher Education or AmDram production.

ISBN 1 902843 10 9

Price: £5.50 each   Set of 15: £70.00

"When our Dan went missing on the 1st January 2002 we assumed that Daniel's face would be absolutely everywhere, appeals on national TV, and everyone would be aware... it wasn't like that for us."

Pauline Nolan (Dan's Mum)

The National Missing Persons Helpline receives more than 100,000 calls every year!!! It helps to resolve 70% of the cases it works on... but 30% remain tragically unresolved.

Dan's family desperately want more media coverage in an attempt to find out where Daniel is.... and so this play was born.

At the time of going to print, Dan is still missing. Please visit his web site www.dan-nolan.co.uk for details of how you may be able to help.

Other Plays by Mark Wheeller

Chunnel of Love

Script: Graham Cole & Mark Wheeller

Duration: 100 mins   **Cast:** 25 (11f, 8m & 6m/f)

A bi-lingual play (80% English & 20% French) about teenage pregnancy. Lucy is fourteen - she hopes to become a vet and is working hard to gain good grades in her GCSE exams, when she discovers she is pregnant. She faces a series of major decisions, not least of which is what to tell the father... Ideal as a school production and Key Stage 4 Drama course book.

Sweet FA !

Script: Mark Wheeller

Duration: 45 mins plus interval   **Cast:** 3f / 2m (or more)

Published by: SchoolPlay Productions Ltd. Tel: 01206 540111

A Zigger Zagger for girls (and boys)! A new play (also available as a full length Musical) telling the true life story of Southampton girl footballer Sarah Stanbury (Sedge) whose ambition is to play Football (Soccer) for England. Her dad is delighted ... her mum disapproves strongly! An ideal GCSE production and Key Stage 4 Drama course book. Drama GCSE scheme of work also available.

Blackout – One Evacuee in Thousands   MUSICAL

Script: Mark Wheeller with the Stantonbury Youth Theatre   **Music:** Mark Wheeller

Duration: 90 mins plus interval   **Published by:** SchoolPlay Productions Ltd.

A Musical about the plight of Rachel Eagle, a fictional evacuee in World War II. Rachel's parents are determined that the war will not split the family up. After refusing to have her evacuated in 1939 they decide to do so midway though 1940. At first Rachel does not settle but, after the death of her mother, she becomes increasingly at home with her billets in Northamptonshire. When her father requests that she return she wants to stay where she feels at home. An ideal large scale school production with good parts for girls (and boys).

The Most Absurd Xmas (Promenade?) Musical in the World...Ever!

Script: Lyndsey Adams, Michael Johnston, Stuart White & Mark Wheeller   **Cast:** Big!

Music: James Holmes   **Duration:** 100 mins

Published by: SchoolPlay Productions Ltd. Tel: 01206 540111

Eat your heart out Ionesco! If you want a musical with a message ... don't consider this one! Santa fails to arrive one year in the Bower of Bliss. Why not? A shortage of carrots perhaps? Or is it because the central character is forbidden to use her musical gift, and whose parents disguise her as a cactus? It all ends reasonably happily and is a bundle of laughs. Originally conceived as a Promenade production. An ideal large scale school Christmas production or alternative an "absurd" summer production.

For more details and an up-to-date list of plays, please visit Mark's website:
www.amdram.co.uk/wheellerplays *(please note wheeller has two "l")*

All enquiries regarding performing rights should be made to: Meg Davis, MBA Literary Agents, 62 Grafton Way, London W1P 5LD. Tel: 020 7387 2076. E-mail: meg@mbalit.co.uk